Unlocking the Power of Mindfulness

Cultivating Resilience and Well-being in the Digital Age

By

Laurel M. West

Table of contents

Introduction

In the present high-speed and interconnected world, the computerized age has achieved tremendous advancement and opened doors. The way we live, work, and connect with others has been transformed by technology, from instant communication to limitless information access. Notwithstanding, alongside these progressions, the advanced age has likewise given us exceptional difficulties that can influence our strength and prosperity.

To navigate the ever-changing digital landscape, resilience—the capacity to adapt and recover from adversity—is essential. It empowers us to endure the tensions and stressors that emerge from steady availability, data overburden, and the requests of our advanced lives. Similarly, living a fulfilled and well-balanced life in the digital age necessitates having a high level of well-being—our overall state of physical, mental, and emotional health.

Developing Strength and Prosperity in the Computerized Age" expects to furnish you with significant bits of knowledge, functional procedures, and care methods to cultivate flexibility and upgrade prosperity amid the difficulties of the advanced world.

All through the accompanying sections, we will investigate the effect of the advanced age on our lives and its advantages and downsides. We will discuss the significance of resilience, its components, and its connection to our overall well-being. By creating versatility, we can all the more likely explore the exceptional stressors and tensions that emerge from living in a computerized society.

The job of careful nurturing at the advanced age will investigate how to raise children who are digitally responsible and equip them with mindfulness and resilience skills to ensure a healthy and balanced relationship with technology from a young age.

In the final section, we will discuss the prospects for well-being and resilience in the digital age. We will consider the potential effects of future technological advancements on our lives and how mindfulness and resilience can assist us in adapting to and thriving in an ever-changing digital environment.

To successfully face the challenges of the digital age, it is essential to cultivate resilience and well-being in today's fast-paced, technology-driven world.

The book begins by looking at how technology affects our lives and the benefits and drawbacks of living in a digital world. It then dives into the requirement for versatility, featuring the different stressors and tensions interesting to the advanced age. The significance of strength in advancing into general prosperity is accentuated.

The center of the digital book centers around developing care as a vital instrument for flexibility. It introduces readers to mindfulness practices designed to control emotions, improve self-awareness, and manage digital distractions. It also offers advice on how to cultivate well-being in the digital age, such as how to practice self-care, keep a work-life balance, and build social connections.

The digital book additionally addresses explicit difficulties of the computerized age, for example, cyberbullying, data over-burden, and inordinate screen time. It offers useful exhortation on building strength to conquer these difficulties and foster solid advanced propensities and limits.

Besides, careful nurturing at the advanced age is investigated, examining procedures for bringing up carefully capable kids and showing them care and strength abilities.

The book comes to a close by looking ahead to possible technological advancements and how they might affect resilience and well-being. By emphasizing the importance of mindfulness and resilience as essential tools, it inspires readers to adapt and thrive in a digital environment that is constantly shifting.

Generally, "Opening the Force of Care: A Comprehensive Guide to Navigating the Digital World with Resilience, mindfulness, and Well-being is provided in the book "Cultivating Resilience and Well-being in the Digital Age."

The Digital Age and the Importance of Resilience and Well-Being In this age where technology is deeply ingrained in our daily lives, cultivating resilience and well-being has taken on a greater significance than ever before. Resilience and well-being are essential for overcoming digital age obstacles for the following reasons:

1. Adapting to Data Overburden: The computerized age has brought a mind-boggling measure of data readily available. We are constantly inundated with information, whether it's via news alerts or updates on social media. Flexibility assists us with sifting through this overburden, focusing on what is significant, and keeping up with mental clearness. Our ability to effectively manage information without feeling overwhelmed or anxious is ensured by our well-being.

2. How to Control Digital Distractions: There are a lot of distractions in the digital world that can make it hard to focus and work efficiently. Strength permits us to keep focused, oppose the enticement of consistent notices, and keep a good overall arrangement between our computerized and disconnected lives. Prosperity outfits us with care strategies and self-guiding abilities to deal with these interruptions and remain present in the assignments that make the biggest difference.

3. Managing the Pressures of social media: Even though it has become an important part of our lives, social media comes with its own set of difficulties. Contrasting ourselves with others, looking for approval through preferences and remarks, and managing cyberbullying are only a couple of instances of the tensions we might encounter in the computerized domain. We can develop a strong sense of self-worth through resilience, resist the negative effects of social media, and keep a positive perspective. We can cultivate genuine connections, establish boundaries, and give our mental and emotional health priority through well-being.

4. Building Computerized Connections: Even though technology lets us connect with people all over the world, it can sometimes make us feel alone and lonely. We can manage the potential difficulties of virtual interactions and the complexities of building and maintaining digital relationships through resilience. Prosperity guarantees that we focus on significant associations, practice sympathy, and participate in solid correspondence in the advanced world.

5. Adjusting Work and Life: The digital age has made the line between work and personal life harder to see. With a consistent network, it very well may be trying to disengage

and find a solid balance between fun and serious activities. We can prioritize self-care, effectively manage our time, and set boundaries with resilience. We are given tools to maintain a

healthy equilibrium through wellness, thereby preventing burnout and enhancing life satisfaction.

6. Adjusting to Mechanical Progressions: The computerized scene is ceaselessly developing, with innovations and stages arising at a quick speed. We can adapt to these changes, embrace innovation, and remain open to the possibilities of the digital age with resilience. The concept of well-being makes certain that we approach these advancements from a healthy perspective, taking into account the impact on our overall health and making conscious decisions that are in line with our values.

In summary, versatility and prosperity are fundamental in the computerized age to adapt to data over-burden, oversee interruptions, explore web-based entertainment pressures, assemble significant associations, balance work and life, and adjust to mechanical progressions. By developing versatility and focusing on prosperity, we can flourish in the computerized world while keeping a solid and satisfying life both on the web and disconnected.

Chapter 1: Understanding the Digital Age

The computerized age alludes to the period in mankind's set of experiences portrayed by the broad use and reconciliation of advanced advances in different parts of society. The way we live, work, communicate, and access information has changed as a result. To better comprehend the digital age, consider these essential points:

1. Technology Developments: The computerized age is set apart by critical headways in innovation, especially in the fields of processing, broadcast communications, and the web. These progressions have prompted the improvement of strong gadgets, for example, cell phones, tablets, and PCs, as well as the production of computerized stages and administrations that have become indispensable to our day-to-day routines.

2. Globalization and connectivity: The globalization and increased connectivity that the digital age has brought is one of its most defining characteristics. The web has associated individuals from all edges of the world, empowering moments of correspondence, joint effort, and the sharing of data on a worldwide scale. The rapid dissemination of ideas, cultures, and knowledge has been made easier by this connectivity.

3. Access to Information: Information is now readily available and abundant in the digital age. With just a few clicks, individuals can access information, research, and educational resources on the Internet, which has developed into a vast repository of knowledge. The way we learn, work, and make decisions has been transformed by this easy access to information.

4. Correspondence and Web-based Entertainment: The way we communicate and interact with others has changed as a result of the digital age. Online entertainment stages, like Facebook, Twitter, and Instagram, have become amazing assets for interfacing, sharing, and communicating our thoughts. We are now able to connect with friends, family, and even strangers from all over the world thanks to these platforms, which have reshaped social dynamics.

5. The Digital Economy: The computerized age has likewise led to the computerized economy, where online organizations, internet businesses, and advanced administrations assume a huge part. Entrepreneurship, remote work, and economic expansion have all benefited from this. Traditional industries like retail, media, and entertainment have also been altered by the digital economy.

6. Problems and worries: The digital age has many advantages, but it also has drawbacks and concerns. Issues, for example, data over-burden, protection breaks, network safety dangers, online badgering, and advanced enslavement have arisen as huge worries. Understanding these difficulties is fundamental to exploring the advanced age securely and mindfully.

7. Continuous Development: The digital age is marked by its continuous development and rapid change rate. How we live and interact with the world is constantly being shaped by new technologies, innovations, and platforms. To succeed in this digital landscape that is constantly changing, you need to be knowledgeable and flexible.

To effectively navigate the challenges of the digital age and take advantage of the opportunities it presents, understanding it is essential. By perceiving the effect of innovation on our lives, we can saddle its true capacity, adjust to changes, and settle on informed choices in this advanced period.

The impact of technology on everyday life:

The way we live, work, communicate, and interact with the world around us has all changed as a result of technology. Here are a few central issues to figure out the effect of innovation on regular daily existence:

1. Communication: Communication has been transformed by technology, making it faster, easier, and more accessible. With the approach of cell phones, virtual entertainment stages, and informing applications, we can immediately associate with individuals across the globe, share data, and take part in continuous discussions.

2. Access to Information: Information access has become more accessible to all. The web has turned into a huge storehouse of information, empowering us to get to data, news, research, and instructive assets with only a couple of snaps. This simple access has changed how we learn, simply decide, and remain informed about the world.

3. Work and Efficiency: The workplace has been significantly impacted by technology, making it more adaptable and efficient. Computerized instruments and programming have smoothed out work processes, robotized errands, and empowered remote work potential open doors. Virtual meetings and global teamwork have been made possible by video conferencing tools and collaboration platforms, removing geographical barriers.

4. Media, Entertainment: Innovation has reformed the amusement and media businesses. Providing instant access to movies, television shows, music, books, streaming services, online platforms, and digital content has disrupted conventional business models. Online entertainment stages have changed how we consume and communicate with media, permitting us to share, remark, and draw in content progressively.

5. Healthcare: Innovation essentially affects medical services, further developing diagnostics, therapy, and patient consideration. Telemedicine, electronic health records, health

monitoring apps and advanced medical devices have made it easier to access healthcare services, made it possible to conduct remote consultations, and made it easier to get personalized care.

6. Travel and Transportation: Innovation has upset transportation and travel, making it more effective and open. The way we plan our trips and navigate cities has been transformed by ride-sharing apps, navigation systems, and real-time updates about transportation. Internet booking stages and travel sites have worked on the most common way of tracking down flights, facilities, and attractions.

7. Personal Lifestyle and Productivity: Innovation has presented many devices and applications that upgrade individual efficiency and way of life. From wellness trackers and shrewd home gadgets to individual accounting applications and time usage instruments, innovation has enabled people to keep tabs on their development, robotize errands, and further develop their general prosperity.

8. Social Elements: Innovation has reshaped social elements, impacting how we collaborate and associate with others. Because they enable us to share experiences, connect with friends and family, and engage with communities of interest, social media platforms have become a primary means of communication. However, it has also sparked concerns regarding privacy, cyberbullying, and the effects of carefully selected online personas on mental health.

Understanding the effect of innovation on daily existence is fundamental to exploring the potential open doors and difficulties it presents. By embracing the advantages while being aware of the possible downsides, we can pursue informed decisions and influence innovation to upgrade our lives in significant ways.

Benefits and challenges of living in a computerized world

Living in a computerized world offers various advantages and open doors, yet it likewise presents novel difficulties. The advantages and disadvantages of living in a digital world are as follows:

Benefits:

1. Connectivity: People from all over the world are now connected via the internet, facilitating instantaneous communication and collaboration. We can interface with companions, family, and partners, paying little heed to geological distance, encouraging a worldwide local area, and working with the trading of thoughts and information.

2. Information Verification: The digital age has made information more accessible to everyone. We can access information, research, educational resources, and news with

just a few clicks thanks to the vast repository of knowledge that the internet provides. This simple admittance to data enables people to learn, go with informed choices, and remain refreshed on a great many themes.

3. Productivity and Comfort: Advanced innovations have made regular undertakings more effective and helpful. From internet shopping and banking to computerized report the board and mechanization instruments, innovation has smoothed out processes, saving time and exertion. We can complete tasks more quickly, access services from the convenience of our homes, and automate tasks that are done over and over again.

4. Worldwide Open doors: Global opportunities for work, education, entrepreneurship, and collaboration have emerged as a result of the digital age. Remote work and web-based learning have become more common, permitting people to work and study from any place. Computerized stages empower business people to contact a worldwide crowd, cultivating development and monetary development.

5. Media, Entertainment: The way we consume and engage with media and entertainment has changed as a result of the digital age. Web-based features, advanced content stages, and virtual entertainment have made it simpler to get to motion pictures, Network programs, music, books, and news. We can customize how much media we consume, interact with creators of content, and share our experiences with others.

Challenges:

1. Overload of information: We are inundated with an overwhelming amount of information in the digital world. It very well may be trying to channel through the huge measure

of content, recognize dependable sources, and stay away from data over-burden. Feelings of overwhelm, disorientation, and difficulty setting priorities can result from the constant flow of information.

2. Computerized Interruptions: Distractions are now more common than ever before thanks to the proliferation of digital platforms and devices. Addiction apps, notifications, and updates from social media can all distract us from our work and reduce productivity. In today's digital world, it is increasingly difficult to focus and control digital distractions.

3. Security and privacy: Privacy and security are two issues that arise from living in a digital world. Information breaks, data fraud, and online tricks are expected dangers. Our own data and online exercises are defenseless, expecting us to be careful about safeguarding our protection and embracing secure practices.

4. Social and Psychological Well-being Effect: The computerized world has changed social elements and can affect emotional wellness. Comparison, FOMO (fear of missing out), and the pressure to create an ideal online persona can all be exacerbated by social media. Cyberbullying and online harassment are also a concern. Offsetting advanced associations with significant up close and personal associations is fundamental for generally speaking prosperity.

5. Digital Gap: Even though technology has become more accessible, there is still a digital divide, which results in disparities in digital literacy and access to technology. There may be disparities in access to essential services, employment opportunities, and education because not everyone enjoys the same opportunities to profit from the digital world.

We can effectively navigate this landscape by comprehending the advantages and disadvantages of living in a digital world. We can make well-informed decisions, develop healthy digital habits, and put our well-being first in the digital age if we take advantage of the advantages while also being aware of the difficulties.

Chapter 2: The Need for Resilience in the Digital Age

Resilience is the ability to bounce back from adversity, adapt to change, and maintain mental and emotional well-being in the face of challenges. In the digital age, where technology is deeply integrated into our lives, the need for resilience becomes even more crucial. Here are some key reasons why resilience is essential in the digital age:

1. Coping with Information Overload: The digital age has brought an unprecedented amount of information to our fingertips. From social media updates to news alerts and emails, we are constantly bombarded with information. Resilience helps us filter through this information overload, prioritize what is truly important, and maintain mental clarity. It enables us to navigate the vast amount of information without feeling overwhelmed or anxious.

2. Managing Digital Distractions: The digital world is filled with distractions that can hinder our productivity and focus. Notifications, social media, and addictive apps can divert our attention and make it challenging to stay on track. Resilience allows us to resist the temptation of constant distractions, maintain self-discipline, and manage our time effectively. It helps us stay focused on our goals and priorities amidst the digital noise.

3. Navigating Social Media Pressures: Social media has become an integral part of our lives, but it also brings its own set of challenges. Comparing ourselves to others, seeking validation through likes and comments, and dealing with cyberbullying are just a few examples of the pressures we may face in the digital realm. Resilience helps us develop a

strong sense of self-worth, resist the negative influences of social media, and maintain a healthy perspective. It enables us to navigate social media in a way that aligns with our values and promotes our well-being.

4. Building Digital Relationships: While technology allows us to connect with others across the globe, it can sometimes lead to a sense of isolation and loneliness. Building and maintaining digital relationships requires resilience. It involves navigating the complexities of virtual interactions, fostering genuine connections, and managing potential challenges such as miscommunication or misunderstandings. Resilience helps us adapt to the nuances of digital relationships, overcome setbacks, and cultivate meaningful connections in the digital world.

5. Balancing Work and Life: The digital age has blurred the boundaries between work and personal life. With constant connectivity, it can be challenging to disconnect and find a healthy work-life balance. Resilience helps us set boundaries, manage our time effectively, and prioritize self-care. It enables us to maintain a healthy equilibrium, preventing burnout and promoting overall life satisfaction.

6. Adapting to Technological Advancements: The digital landscape is continuously evolving, with new technologies and platforms emerging at a rapid pace. Resilience is essential to adapt to these changes. It helps us embrace innovation, stay open-minded, and navigate the uncertainties that come with technological advancements. Resilience enables us to embrace new technologies, acquire new skills, and thrive in the ever-changing digital world.

In summary, resilience is crucial in the digital age to cope with information overload, manage distractions, navigate social media pressures, build digital relationships, balance work and life, and adapt to technological advancements. By cultivating resilience, we can effectively navigate the challenges of the digital age, maintain our well-being, and thrive in the ever-evolving digital landscape.

Definition and parts of flexibility

Flexibility is the capacity to adjust, return, and keep up with prosperity notwithstanding affliction, challenges, or critical life stressors. It involves being able to recover and thrive in the face of challenging circumstances. Resilience is a set of skills, attitudes, and behaviors that can be learned and improved over time, rather than a single trait. Resilience consists primarily of the following elements:

1. Regulating one's emotions: The capacity to effectively recognize, comprehend, and manage one's emotions is referred to as emotional regulation. Resilient people are adept at recognizing their feelings, healthily expressing them, and managing strong emotions to keep them from taking over their well-being. They have techniques to adapt to pressure, uneasiness, and other pessimistic feelings, permitting them to explore difficulties with close-to-home steadiness.

2. Positive Perspective and Optimism: Versatile people will more often than not have a hopeful and inspirational perspective on life. They believe they can overcome obstacles and keep their hope alive by focusing on the possibilities. They can reframe challenges as opportunities for growth, keep a sense of purpose, and approach challenging circumstances with resilience and determination when they are optimistic.

3. Critical thinking Abilities: Having strong problem-solving skills is necessary for resilience. Versatile people are proactive in recognizing and tending to difficulties. They have a lot of ideas, are flexible, and can come up with good solutions to problems. Instead of dwelling on the issue itself, they approach difficulties with a mindset that emphasizes locating solutions.

4. Social Help and Association: Strength is cultivated through friendly help and association. Versatile people have major areas of strength for an organization of family, companions, or networks that offer close-to-home help, consolation, and help during troublesome times. They are also adept at seeking and accepting assistance when required and understanding the significance of social connections in overcoming obstacles.

5. Taking care of oneself and prosperity: Self-care and well-being are two of the most important aspects of resilience. Versatile people comprehend the significance of dealing with their physical, mental, and close-to-home well-being. They take part in exercises that advance prosperity, like activity, care, good dieting, and sufficient rest. They maintain their overall health and resilience by prioritizing self-care.

6. Versatility and Adaptability: Versatility includes being versatile and adaptable, notwithstanding change and vulnerability. Resilient people are open to new experiences, ideas, and points of view. When the situation calls for it, they can alter their plans and expectations, allowing them to overcome obstacles and setbacks.

7. Growth Mentality: Strong people have a development mentality, which is the conviction that capacities and insight can be created through exertion and learning. Instead of being

fixed limitations, they see challenges as opportunities for growth and learning. They can accept setbacks, gain knowledge from mistakes, and continuously improve themselves as a result of this mindset.

Together, these aspects of resilience assist individuals in overcoming obstacles, navigating adversity, and maintaining

well-being. By developing these abilities and mentalities, people can reinforce their versatility and flourish despite life's troubles.

Common stressors and pressures in the Digital Age

There are several common stressors and pressures that people frequently encounter in the digital age. Here are a few key ones:

1. Inundation of information: People frequently experience feelings of being overwhelmed as a result of the vast amount of information at their disposal, and they find it challenging to remain current and make sense of the constant influx of data.

2. Computerized network: While innovation considers an expanded network, it can likewise prompt sensations of consistent accessibility and the assumptions for moment reactions, prompting pressure and an absence of balance between serious and fun activities.

3. Virtual entertainment correlations: Online entertainment stages can add to deep-seated insecurities, as people frequently contrast their lives with cautiously arranged profiles of others. Stress and low self-esteem are possible outcomes of this.

4. Cyberbullying and online provocation: The digital age has brought about a variety of forms of online harassment that can have serious emotional repercussions and cause anxiety and stress.

5. FOMO, or the fear of missing out: Web-based entertainment stages open people to the exercises and encounters of others, prompting an apprehension about passing up occasions, social events, or open doors, which can bring about pressure and tension.

6. Unreasonable assumptions for efficiency: Innovation and consistent availability can assume nonstop efficiency. This strain to constantly be useful can prompt burnout and persistent pressure.

7. Problems with digital security: Concerns about digital security and privacy have become significant sources of stress as more aspects of our lives are conducted online. Managing passwords or safeguarding personal information are everyday tasks that can cause anxiety.

To maintain mental well-being in the digital age, it is essential to be aware of these stressors and develop coping mechanisms like setting boundaries, taking breaks from technology, practicing self-care, and seeking support when needed.

The link between resilience and well-being

Versatility and prosperity are interconnected ideas. Versatility alludes to a singular's capacity to adjust and return from difficulties, affliction, or stress. On the other hand, a more comprehensive sense of one's overall health, happiness, and contentment in life are all parts of well-being.

Resilience helps one cope with life's challenges and maintain a positive mental and emotional state, which is the link between resilience and well-being. Resilient people are better able to deal with setbacks, stress, and uncertainty, which can have a positive effect on their overall health.

People can better manage stress, maintain a positive outlook, and develop effective coping mechanisms by developing resilience. This, generally, advances a feeling of prosperity by encouraging close-to-home equilibrium, flexibility, and the capacity to track down importance and fulfillment in different parts of life. In this way, the development of versatility assumes an urgent part in advancing and supporting general prosperity.

Chapter 3: Cultivating Mindfulness for Resilience

Mindfulness training can be a potent tool for building resilience. The practice of paying deliberate, non-judgmental attention to the present moment is referred to as mindfulness. It permits people to be completely present and mindful of their viewpoints, feelings, and sensations. Here is an overall outline of how developing care can add to versatility:

1. Creating mindfulness: Mindfulness helps people become more aware of what they are thinking, feeling, and doing. They can more easily identify their stressors, triggers, and behavior patterns as a result of this self-awareness. By understanding oneself better, people can answer all the more to difficulties and assemble strength.

2. Managing anxiety: An attitude of acceptance and non-judgment toward internal experiences is fostered through mindfulness. People who engage in mindfulness can approach stressful or difficult situations with greater calm and clarity. They can observe their thoughts and feelings without becoming swept up in them, which lessens the impact that stress has on their well-being.

3. Improving close-to-home guidelines: Care assists people with turning out to be more sensitive to their feelings and fosters a capacity to answer as opposed to responding incautiously. By distinguishing and recognizing their feelings without judgment, people can pick how to answer in a more versatile and strong way, even in testing circumstances.

4. Building concentration and fixation: Care works out, like reflection or careful breathing, to fortify consideration and concentration. This better center permits people to remain present even with interruptions and focus on the job needing to be done. People become more resilient and adept at overcoming challenges when they develop this skill.

5. Making self-compassion a priority: Mindfulness inspires people to treat themselves with kindness and compassion. Adopting a growth mindset and accepting one's limitations are two aspects of self-compassion. By treating oneself with consideration and understanding, people can return from misfortunes all the more effectively and foster more noteworthy flexibility.

6. Advancing generally speaking prosperity: Ordinary care practice has been related with various advantages for by and large prosperity, including decreased tension and gloom, worked on mental capability, and better pressure the board. Individuals increase their resilience by taking care of their well-being. This strengthens their capacity to adapt to difficulties and setbacks.

Developing care for versatility includes integrating care rehearses in everyday existence, like reflection, careful breathing activities, or being more present in regular exercises. Individuals can cultivate a mindset and set of skills that support greater resilience in the face of adversity over time with consistent practice.

Benefits of Mindfulness

Care is a training that includes purposefully focusing on the current second, without judgment. It involves paying attention to our thoughts, emotions, and bodily sensations as well as the environment around us. Here is an overall outline of the prologue to Care and its advantages:

1. Present-moment awareness: Mindfulness helps us focus on the here and now by bringing our attention back to the here and

now. Mindfulness encourages us to fully experience and appreciate the present moment rather than dwelling on the past or worrying about the future.

2. Awareness without bias: The practice of mindfulness encourages us to observe our feelings, thoughts, and sensations without judging or criticizing them. It trains us to acknowledge things as they are, cultivating self-sympathy and lessening superfluous self-judgment.

3. Stress decrease: Stress reduction is one of mindfulness's most well-known advantages. By zeroing in on the current second and practicing non-reactivity, care assists us in exploring unpleasant circumstances with greater lucidity and serenity.

4. Work on close-to-home prosperity: By increasing our awareness of our own emotions as well as the emotions of others, mindfulness improves emotional intelligence. It permits us to more readily direct our feelings, further developing our, by and large, profound prosperity and flexibility.

5. enhanced mental performance: Normal care practices have been displayed to work on mental capability, including consideration, memory, and critical thinking skills. It can build concentration and fixation, prompting further developed efficiency and execution.

6. Better connections: Empathy and compassion are developed through mindfulness, which enables us to be more present and attentive when interacting with other people. It promotes effective communication and conflict resolution by fostering deeper connections and understanding in relationships.

7. Benefits for the body's health: Care has been related to different actual medical advantages, for example, diminished circulatory strain, worked safe capability, diminished torment insight, better rest, and by and large prosperity.

8. self-awareness raised: Care assists us with fostering a more profound comprehension of ourselves by seeing our themes of reasoning and responding. It carries attention to our qualities, convictions, and inspirations, supporting self-awareness and self-disclosure.

9. Versatility and flexibility: Mindfulness improves our capacity to overcome obstacles and setbacks by fostering present-moment awareness and acceptance without judging. It advances flexibility and versatility despite the difficulty.

10. Overall happiness: The holistic practice of mindfulness has positive effects on all facets of our lives—physical, mental, emotional, and interpersonal. It brings a feeling of harmony, balance, and expanded by and large prosperity.

Start by incorporating simple practices like mindful breathing, body scans, and mindful eating into your daily routine to reap the benefits of mindfulness. With reliable practice, care turns into an approach to being that changes our relationship with ourselves and our general surroundings.

Mindfulness procedures for managing computerized interruptions

Overseeing computerized interruptions through care procedures can be exceptionally advantageous in keeping up with centers, decreasing pressure, and further developing efficiency. The following are some mindfulness practices that are specifically designed to manage digital distractions:

1. Tech restrictions should be deliberate: Begin by establishing deliberate limits on your use of technology. Assign explicit times during the day for browsing messages, virtual entertainment, or other computerized exercises. Consider turning off notifications or using dedicated apps or browser extensions that block websites or apps that are distracting during focused work or important tasks to minimize interruptions.

2. Be mindful when using technology: Before drawing in with computerized gadgets or stages, pause for a minute to respite and set a goal for your use. Consider the connection between the app or device you're using and your priorities. Carry cognizant attention to your activities, limiting thoughtless looking over or meandering through applications.

3. Planned Breaks: Plan deliberate breaks to take a look at computerized gadgets.

Make mindful use of these breaks, paying attention to their purpose and duration.

4. Single-Tasking: Center around each assignment in turn.

To reduce digital overload and improve concentration, refrain from multitasking.

5. Careful Application Usage: Define specific checking times for apps. Use apps with care and refrain from mindless scrolling.

6. Awareness of the digital environment: Set up your digital workspace in a thoughtful way. To reduce temptations, remove unnecessary shortcuts or applications.

You can effectively manage distractions and cultivate a more intentional and focused approach to your digital interactions by incorporating these mindfulness techniques.

Building mindfulness and profound guidelines

Building mindfulness and upgrading close-to-home guidelines are significant abilities that add to self-improvement and prosperity. Here are some moves toward assist you with fostering these abilities:

Building Awareness of Oneself:

1. Reflection: Schedule regular time for self-reflection. Consider journaling or just saving calm minutes to ponder your contemplations, sentiments, and activities.

2. Practices in Mindfulness: To bring your attention to the present moment and increase your self-awareness, engage in mindfulness activities like meditation or deep breathing exercises.

3. Input Seeking: Look for valuable criticism from confided-in companions, family, or associates. Your thoughts and actions can be better understood from outside perspectives.

4. Journaling Your Feelings: To keep track of your feelings throughout the day, keep an emotional journal. To gain a

better understanding of your emotional responses, look for patterns and triggers.

5. Character Assessments: Take personality tests or self-discovery tools to learn more about your preferences, strengths, and areas for improvement.

Building mindfulness and upgrading profound guidelines is a continuous interaction. Be patient with yourself, celebrate your progress, and commit to ongoing improvement in your ability to comprehend and control your emotions.

Chapter 4: Sustaining Prosperity in the Advanced Age

Sustaining prosperity in the computerized age includes an all-encompassing methodology that considers physical, mental, and close-to-home perspectives. Some suggestions:

1. Establish Digital Limits: Define specific usage times for the device. Designate times of the day and place in your home where you won't use technology.

2. Practice mindfulness: Consolidate care strategies to oversee pressure. Participate fully and fully present in non-digital moments.

3. Computerized Detox: Enjoy normal reprieves from screens. Plan periodic days without computerized gadgets to re-energize.

4. Focus on Sleep: Set a routine for going to bed without using electronic devices. For better quality sleep, limit time spent in front of a screen before bedtime.

5. Develop True Connections: Balance on the web and disconnected social associations. Support face-to-face connections for a feeling of the local area.

You can cultivate a healthier relationship with technology and promote overall well-being in the digital age by incorporating these practices into your lifestyle.

Importance of self-care in the advanced world

The significance of taking care of oneself in the advanced world is foremost because of the special difficulties and requests presented by our rising dependence on innovation. Here are the key reasons featuring its importance:

1. Stress and digital overload: In the advanced age, consistent availability and data over-burden can prompt uplifted feelings of anxiety. Taking care of oneself goes about as an essential cradle against computerized stressors, helping people oversee and reduce the strain related to computerized requests.

2. Eye strain and screen fatigue: Eye strain, exhaustion, and other physical discomforts can all be brought on by prolonged screen time. To lessen the physical impact of excessive screen time, self-care practices like taking frequent breaks, performing eye exercises, and making ergonomic adjustments are essential.

3. Mental Well-being: Mental health can be affected by constant exposure to social media, online news, and digital communication. Taking care of oneself schedules, including care rehearses, assists with keeping a solid mental state by giving snapshots of unwinding and profound equilibrium.

4. Quality of Sleep: Using electronic devices excessively, particularly before bedtime, can disrupt sleep patterns. Focusing on taking care of oneself

includes laying out solid rest cleanliness, advancing better rest quality, and guaranteeing sufficient rest.

Generally, taking care of oneself in the computerized world is a proactive and fundamental way to deal with saving and improving by and large prosperity. It fosters a healthy and long-lasting relationship with the digital landscape by empowering individuals to maximize the benefits of technology while minimizing its potential drawbacks.

Strategies for keeping a healthy work-life balance

Systems for Keeping a Solid Balance between fun and serious activities:

1. Layout Boundaries: Set clear work hours that don't overlap with personal time. Set assumptions with associates and bosses regarding your accessibility beyond work hours.

2. Focus on Tasks: Identify and rank tasks in order of importance and urgency. Set aside time during designated work hours to complete high-priority tasks.

3. Blocking of time: Set aside specific time slots for breaks, personal pursuits, and work. To establish a structured routine, adhere to the schedule.

4. Learn how to say no: Survey your responsibility and responsibilities all things considered. When you already have too much on your plate, be willing to decline additional tasks.

5. Make a Committed Workspace: To keep work and personal life separate, create a designated workspace. At the end of the day, leave your work area to disconnect mentally.

6. Set Reasonable Goals: Set goals for your work and personal lives that are attainable and attainable. Don't make too much and you won't feel overwhelmed.

7. Turn off During Individual Time: During personal time, disconnect from work-related messages and emails. Use "Don't Upset" highlights on gadgets to limit interferences.

8. Pause frequently: Plan brief breaks during the average working day to re-energize. To maintain focus, take breaks for physical activity or relaxation.

Increasing social connections and decreasing feelings of isolation Increasing social connections and decreasing feelings of isolation necessitates making proactive efforts to establish and uphold meaningful relationships. Some methods include:

1. Join Clubs or Groups: Join clubs or groups to do the things you enjoy. Make new friends who are interested in the same things as you are.

2. Go to Social Events: Participate in meetups, social gatherings, or community events. Partake in neighborhood exercises to grow your group of friends.

3. Attend workshops or classes: Sign up for classes or studios to acquire new abilities. Make connections with people whose learning goals are similar.

4. Be Available to New Relationships: Be open-minded in social situations. Start discussions and make new companions.

5. Make use of technology to meet new people: Make new friends or reconnect with old ones by using social media. Look into online communities that are related to your interests or hobbies.

Keep in mind that it takes time and effort to make social connections. Show restraint toward yourself as well as other people as you explore these connections. Since quality matters more than quantity, concentrate on cultivating meaningful relationships.

Chapter 5: Building Resilience in the face of digital challenges

Building flexibility despite computerized difficulties includes creating versatile methodologies and a positive mentality. Here is an aide:

1. Practices in Mindfulness: To remain present and focused in the face of digital distractions, incorporate mindfulness practices. Practice care contemplation to upgrade your capacity to answer smoothly to difficulties.

2. Embrace a growth mindset: See difficulties as opportunities for development and learning. Treat setbacks as stepping stones toward improvement and consider them to be temporary.

3. Enhance your emotional intelligence: Acquire self-awareness and an understanding of how you react emotionally to digital challenges. In online interactions, learn to effectively manage emotions and empathize with others.

4. Set Reasonable Goals: Lay out reachable objectives that take into consideration consistent advancement. Divide more complex tasks into manageable steps.

5. Acquire the ability to solve problems: Increase your capacity for digital problem-solving analysis. Look for proactive solutions and approach difficulties as puzzles to be solved.

6. Establish a Support Group: For support, cultivate relationships both online and offline. Make connections with people who share your interests and can offer advice and support.

7. Flexibility in Change: In the face of rapid technological change, be flexible. Keep your skills current and adapt to new platforms and tools.

8. Time Management: To effectively manage digital overload, prioritize tasks. To avoid burnout, limit your screen time.

9. Consider Resilience: Consider how resilient you are in the face of digital obstacles regularly. Choose the tactics that work best for you and modify them accordingly.

10. Tech Detox Moments: Plan regular breaks from electronic devices. Engage in non-work activities during these times to recharge and gain perspective.

You can strengthen your resilience in the face of digital obstacles by incorporating these practices, fostering a positive and adaptable approach to the changing digital landscape.

Dealing with cyberbullying and online badgering

Managing cyberbullying and online badgering requires a blend of proactive measures and compelling reactions. How to deal with these kinds of situations:

1. Be calm and evaluate: Before responding, take a moment to regain your composure. Evaluate the situation's severity and potential impact on your health.

2. Try not to Draw in Negatively: Try not to answer with outrage or antagonism. Avoid fighting back, as this can raise what is happening.

3. Take note of the Harassment: Document the messages or content that is offensive. Take screen captures and save any applicable data as proof.

4. Utilize the Privacy Options: Check and make changes to your social media account's privacy settings. Limit the data noticeable to people in general.

5. Report and Block: Block the involved parties to prevent further communication. Report the badgering to the individual stage or site.

6. Look for Support: Discuss the matter with friends, family, or coworkers. For emotional support, share your experience with someone you trust.

7. Inform those in charge: Inform law enforcement of the harassment if it involves threats or illegal activities. Present them with the documented evidence.

8. Education on Internet Safety: Learn about online safety precautions for yourself. Discover how to identify and ward off potential dangers.

Keep in mind that your health is important. Feel free to help, whether it's from companions, family, or experts. Make use of the resources and tools available on online platforms to address and combat cyberbullying.

Managing information overload and digital overwhelm

To maintain focus, reduce stress, and cultivate a healthy relationship with technology, managing information overload and digital overwhelm is essential. You can use the following practical strategies to get through these obstacles:

1. Focus on and Set Goals: Set clear objectives and prioritize your top priorities. Center around errands that line up with your targets to try not to feel overpowered by superfluous data.

2. Advanced Detox: Plan standard computerized detox periods where you detach from screens. Your mind can reset during this break, reducing the constant influx of information.

3. Restrict Notifications to Impair trivial warnings on your gadgets. Pick just the main alarms to limit interference and keep up with the center.

4. Organize the Data: Effectively organize information by utilizing digital tools. To make it easier to find emails, documents, and other digital content, create folders, labels, or tags.

5. Blocking of time: Allocate specific time slots for various tasks using time-blocking strategies. Concentration is improved and multitasking is prevented.

6. Set Data Boundaries: Set clear limits on the times and places you consume information. Don't read or listen to information before bedtime, for example.

7. Declutter and unsubscribe: Withdraw from bulletins and warnings that don't enhance your life. Routinely clean up your advanced space by erasing or chronicling superfluous documents.

8. Use Efficiency Tools: Influence efficiency devices and applications that assist with smoothing out your work process. Applications for the calendar, note-taking, and task management can help with organization.

9. Mindfully use technology: Be mindful of your use of digital media. Enjoy reprieves between screen meetings, and practice deliberate commitment as opposed to thoughtless looking over.

10. Channel Data Sources: Locate reliable and pertinent informational sources. Channel your memberships, follow believable sites, and curate your computerized feed to keep away from data over-burden.

11. Learn how to say no: Perceive your cutoff points and express no to extra undertakings, ventures, or data that might add to overpower.

12. Cluster Processing: Combine similar tasks in a batch process. For instance, commit explicit times for answering messages, messages, or virtual entertainment refreshes as opposed to tending to them inconsistently.

13. Perform extensive work: Take part in profound work meetings where you center around a solitary errand without interruptions. This further develops efficiency and lessens the feeling of computerized overpowering.

14. Attainable Expectations: Set yourself goals that you can meet. Accept that you won't be able to process or absorb all of the information at your disposal.

15. Invest in ongoing education: Improve your ability to process information. To effectively filter and absorb relevant information, cultivate your capacity for critical thinking and discernment.

Keep in mind that information overload management is an ongoing process. Try different things with various procedures to find what turns out best for you, and be versatile as your requirements and conditions develop. Routinely survey and change your computerized propensities to keep a good arrangement.

Creating solid computerized propensities and limits

Creating solid computerized propensities and limits includes careful practices and deliberate decisions. Here are some steps you can take to improve your relationship with technology:

1. Clear Objectives: Set goals for how you want to use digital devices. Decide what you want to accomplish both professionally and personally.
2. Make a schedule online: Dedicate a specific amount of time to digital activities.

Characterize periods for work, online entertainment, and recreation.

3. Make offline activities a priority: Make time for things that don't involve technology. Spend time with loved ones, exercise, or engage in hobbies away from screens.

4. Mindful time spent online. Choose your screen time wisely. Keep away from careless looking over and set time limits for certain applications.

5. Stop receiving notifications: Tweak notice settings to limit interruptions. Switch off insignificant notices during centered work or individual time.

6. Assess Application Usage: Audit your application use consistently. Get rid of apps that waste time or distract you.

7. Apply the 20-20-20 Method: To lessen eye strain, adhere to the 20-20-20 rule. Look at something 20 feet away for at least 20 seconds every 20 minutes.

8. Set Work Boundaries: Set clear working hours and stick to them. Inform coworkers of your availability, and refrain from responding to emails sent during business hours.

9. Learn for yourself: Stay up to date on the effects of too much screen time. Recognize the significance of digital well-being and the effects it has on mental health.

10. Monitor Your Use of social media: Don't spend too much time on social media. Don't follow accounts that make you feel bad or compare yourself to others.

11. Introduce Rituals Free of Technology: Have rituals without technology. Spend less time in front of a screen doing things like reading or practicing relaxation techniques.

You can cultivate a healthier digital lifestyle by putting these methods into practice. This will help you strike a balance between the benefits of technology and your overall health.

Chapter 6: Mindful parenting and digital well-being

The application of mindfulness principles to the way parents navigate and manage their children's interaction with digital devices is the basis of mindful parenting in the context of digital well-being. Here is a summary:

Careful Parenting:

An approach known as mindful parenting applies mindfulness principles to both the difficulties and pleasures of raising children. Being completely present, not judging, and paying attention to your child's needs, feelings, and experiences are all part of it. With their children, mindful parents cultivate awareness, emotional regulation, and open communication.

Digital Health:

Maintaining a healthy and balanced relationship with digital devices and online activities is referred to as digital well-being. It involves mindfully using technology to minimize potential adverse effects on physical, mental, and emotional health. Strategies for controlling screen time, developing healthy tech habits, and creating a positive online environment are all part of digital well-being.

Parents can help their children develop a healthy and balanced relationship with technology by integrating mindful parenting practices and a focus on digital well-being.

Navigating the difficulties of raising children in the computerized age

Exploring the difficulties of bringing kids up in the computerized age requires a smart and proactive methodology. Consider the following options to help you:

- Learn for yourself: Stay up to date on technological advancements and the digital landscape. Recognize the advantages and disadvantages of various online platforms.
- Communicating openly: Encourage children to communicate honestly and openly with you. Urge them to share their web-based encounters, questions, and concerns.
- Layout Clear Guidelines: Set clear principles and rules regarding screen time, online exercises, and gadget utilization. Team up with your youngsters to lay out age-proper limits.
- Model Solid Tech Habits: As a parent, demonstrate responsible and mindful use of technology. Set an example of how to use the computer and the internet healthily.
- Online safety education: Instruct your kids about internet-based security, protection, and the expected dangers of sharing individual data. Impart the significance of dependable computerized conduct.
- Energize Basic Thinking: Help children evaluate online content by developing their

critical thinking skills. Teach them to question information, identify false information, and make well-informed choices.

- Connect Online: Participate in digital activities as a family. Engage in online learning, educational games, and age-appropriate content.
- Observe Online Activity: Pay attention to your child's online activities and platforms. Utilize parental controls and observing instruments to guarantee a safe web-based climate.
- Empower Disconnected Activities: Advance harmony among on the web and disconnected exercises. To promote a balanced lifestyle, encourage hobbies, sports, and face-to-face interactions.
- Educate Advanced Empathy: Instill a sense of kindness and empathy in online interactions. Talk about how others are affected by digital words and actions.
- Maintain Engagement in Education: Team up with your kid's school to figure out their way to deal with innovation. Remain engaged with their computerized instruction and backing drives advancing dependable tech use.
- Layout Without Tech Zones: Designate specific times or areas of the home as tech-free. Give your family chances to spend quality time together without screens.

- Address Cyberbullying: Show your youngster how to perceive and answer cyberbullying. If they report any incidents of bullying, you should take the necessary measures.
- Remain Associated with Peers: Be aware of your child's interactions with others, both online and offline. Help peers make positive social connections.
- Adapt your parenting methods: Be adaptable and adjust your nurturing techniques as your kid develops and innovation advances. Maintain your interest and keep learning about new digital issues and trends.

Keep in mind that a supportive environment and open communication are essential. Consistently reconsider and change your methodology in light of your kid's age, development, and the advancing computerized scene.

Maintaining healthy boundaries and fostering digital balance

Maintaining a healthy relationship with technology and establishing healthy boundaries requires deliberate strategies to ensure a harmonious relationship. To achieve this, take the following concrete steps:

- Delineate boundaries: Set clear guidelines for how to use your device. Characterize explicit times for sans-tech exercises and assigned screen time.

- Establish tech-free areas: Assign specific regions or times in your home as sans tech zones. Elevate up close and personal collaborations without the interruption of screens.
- Layout Family Tech Guidelines: Create tech guidelines together with family members. Make sure that everyone agrees to the boundaries that have been set.
- Be an example of good health: As a parent or caregiver, demonstrate responsible use of technology. Show that you prioritize offline activities and practice moderation in your screen time.
- Boost Outdoor Recreation: Encourage outdoor play and physical activity. Maintain a healthy balance between screen time and opportunities to exercise and explore the outdoors.
- Make use of parental controls: Make use of devices' parental control options. Set age-proper limitations to screen and restrict content.
- Inform people about online safety: Instruct members of your family about online security and privacy. Examine possible dangers and fitting web-based conduct.
- Plan family time without technology: Make devoted sans tech family minutes. Participate in exercises that encourage genuine associations and quality time together.

- Layout Screen Time Routines: Establish regular schedules for screen time. Schedule specific times online for socializing, entertainment, and educational content.
- Encourage Activities Offline: Empower side interests and exercises that don't include screens. Support the advancement of disconnected interests and abilities.
- Maintain a balance between personal and professional use of technology: Lay out clear limits for work and individual tech use. Define specific times to respond to calls and emails from work.
- Mindfully use technology: Be aware of your tech use propensities. Stay away from thoughtless looking over and survey the reason for each internet-based communication.
- Assess Application Usage: Consistently audit the applications and stages you use. Eliminate or restrict applications that add to computerized overpower.
- Schedule time off from technology: Define specific times when you won't use technology. Utilize this chance to participate in exercises that advance unwinding and prosperity.
- Routinely Evaluate and Adjust: Check on the effectiveness of the established boundaries regularly. Make changes to the rules in response to changes in technology or family dynamics.

By carrying out these methodologies, you establish a climate that advances sound tech propensities and guarantees a fair utilization of computerized gadgets inside your loved ones. Normal correspondence and adaptability are fundamental for adjusting these rules to the developing requirements of your family.

Showing care and strength abilities to kids

Showing care and strength abilities to kids includes integrating age-fitting practices that advance profound prosperity and versatility. Some effective methods include:

- Lead by Example: In your actions, show that you are mindful. Set an example of resilience by overcoming obstacles calmly and cheerfully.
- Focus on your breathing: Acquaint straightforward breathing activities with assistance to kids centered around their breath. Show them how to take deep, deliberate breaths when they are stressed.
- Utilize Careful Games and Activities: Involve children in mindfulness-based activities like yoga, meditation, or mindful coloring. Make it fun by consolidating games that include cantered consideration and unwinding.
- Make Mindful Listening a Practice: Show the significance of listening mindfully. Engage children in mindful listening activities that require them to concentrate on various sounds in the environment.

- Manifest Your Thanks: Inspire a sense of gratitude in children by encouraging them to share their feelings of gratitude. Make an everyday or week-by-week appreciation routine to feature positive parts of their lives.
- Teach Emotional Intelligence: Assist children in recognizing and expressing their feelings. To help people talk about how they feel, use tools like emotion charts or drawings.
- Encourage Self-Care: Help kids to be thoughtful to themselves during testing times. Inspire self-love and positive self-talk.
- Read books on mindfulness: Through age-appropriate books, introduce concepts of mindfulness and resilience. To improve comprehension, talk about the lessons and stories.
- Eating mindfully: Practice mindful eating habits. Inspire children to appreciate the flavors and textures of their food and to savor each bite.

Chapter 7 Future of resilience and well-being in the Digital Age

The fate of versatility and prosperity in the computerized age is probably going to be molded by continuous progressions in innovation, cultural changes, and developing familiarity with the significance of psychological wellness. Considerations and possible trends include:

1. Integration of Technology for Health: The development of new digital apps and tools that specifically support mental health and well-being is continuing. The incorporation of artificial intelligence (AI) for individualized recommendations and treatments for well-being.

2. Mindfulness in Virtual and Augmented Reality: Expanding utilization of virtual and increased reality for vivid care encounters. Virtual reality (VR) and augmented reality (AR) applications that aid in relaxation and stress reduction.

3. Insights Driven by Data: The expanding application of data analytics to the purpose of providing individuals with insights into their well-being.

Customized proposals are given information gathered from wearables and advanced communications.

4. Advanced Emotional Wellness Platforms: The expansion of online mental health counseling, therapy, and resources on digital mental health platforms. Expanded openness to emotional wellness support through telehealth administrations.

5. Mindful Technology Design Proceeded with accentuation on careful innovation plan to diminish computerized interruptions and advance positive client encounters. Joining prosperity highlights in computerized items to help clients in overseeing screen time.

6. Instructive Programs: Incorporating well-being and resilience education into school curriculums. Accentuation on showing computerized locals how to explore the advanced scene while keeping up with mental and close-to-home well-being.

7. Corporate Prosperity Initiatives: A growing emphasis on programs for workplace well-being, including digital resources and tools. Initiatives by the company to address the negative effects of digital stress on the mental health of employees.

8. Preventative Measures for Mental Health: Move toward measures that prevent mental illness, such as early intervention strategies. Expanded mindfulness and comprehension of the significance of proactive emotional wellness care.

9. Technologies for Assisted Therapy: Progressions in tech-helped treatment, including the utilization of virtual advisors and chatbots. Coordination of simulated intelligence-driven helpful intercessions for different psychological well-being conditions.

10. Moves in the Digital Detox: Proceeded with mindfulness and promotion for advanced detox rehearses. Social movements that encourage mindful use of technology and regular breaks from it.
11. Research on Computerized Impact: Constant investigation into the long-term effects of digital technologies on mental health. The creation of guidelines for healthy digital habits based on evidence.
12. Awareness of Global Well-Being: Making people all over the world more aware of how important mental health and well-being are. Group efforts to address the societal issue of digital well-being.

In the digital age, a holistic approach that combines technology, education, policy, and individual responsibility will likely play a crucial role as we move forward. A healthier and more resilient relationship with digital technologies will result from advocacy for digital well-being, ethical tech practices, and a supportive societal framework.

Potential innovative progressions and their effect

Surely, mechanical headways can essentially influence different parts of our lives. Some potential developments and their effects are as follows:

1. Computerized reasoning (man-made intelligence) and Machine Learning: Effect: Mechanization of errands, customized suggestions, and further developed direction. [Perspectives:] concerns about ethics, job loss, and data privacy.

2. Technology for 5G:

Effect: Quicker web speeds, low-dormancy correspondence, improved availability for IoT.

Considerations: Framework prerequisites, potential well-being concerns.

3. Virtual Reality (VR) and augmented reality (AR):

Effect: Vivid encounters in gaming, schooling, medical care, and work environment preparation.

[Perspectives:] Integrity issues, the possibility of addiction, and privacy concerns

4. Web of Things (IoT):

Effect: improved data collection, resource management efficiency, and connected smart devices

Considerations: Security gambles, protection issues, normalization challenges.

5. Technology for the Blockchain:

Impact: Decentralized systems, and transactions that are safe and open.

Considerations: energy consumption, scalability issues, and regulatory obstacles

6. Genetic coding and biotechnology:

Effect: advances in disease prevention, personalized medicine, and gene therapy.

Considerations: Moral problems, expected abuse, worries about hereditary protection.

7. Robotics:

Impact: Robotization in assembling, medical care, and administration enterprises.

Considerations: Work dislodging, moral utilization of independent frameworks.

8. Technologies for Clean Energies:

Impact: Supportable energy sources, decreased ecological effect.

[Perspectives:] Starting expense, mix difficulties, asset accessibility.

9. 3D Printing:

 Effect: Tweaked producing, quick prototyping, clinical applications.

[Perspectives:] Licensed innovation concerns, material impediments, administrative issues.

10. Neurotechnology:

Impact: advancements in neurological treatments and brain-machine interfaces.

[Perspectives:] Privacy concerns, ethical considerations, and the possibility of misuse.

11. Computing at the edge

Impact: Quicker handling of information at the edge of the organization, diminished dormancy.

[Perspectives:] Security challenges, normalization issues.

These advancements have advantages as well as drawbacks, highlighting the necessity of ethical considerations, effective regulation, and responsible development to ensure a positive impact on society.

Strategies for adapting to and thriving in a digital landscape

Adapting to and thriving in a digital landscape that is always changing requires a proactive and adaptable approach. Strategies for successfully navigating the dynamic digital environment include:

- Persistent Learning: Keep up with the latest industry trends and emerging technologies. To stay relevant, invest in ongoing education and skill development.
- Accept Change: Foster a mentality that invites change as a chance for development. Be versatile and open to better approaches for working and thinking.
- Collaboration and networking: Establish a robust professional network offline as well as online. To gain new perspectives and insights, collaborate with a variety of people.
- Thinking Ahead: Develop nimble reasoning and critical thinking abilities. Be prepared to

pivot and modify tactics in response to changing circumstances.

- Computerized Literacy: Upgrade advanced proficiency abilities to explore new apparatuses and innovations. Recognize the effects that digital advancements will have on your sector.
- Mentality of an entrepreneur: Foster a pioneering outlook that values advancement. Investigate amazing open doors for making worth and tackling issues.
- Time Management: To effectively manage digital overload, prioritize tasks. To avoid burnout, limit your screen time.
- Develop Resilience: Develop emotional resilience to overcome obstacles. Gain from mishaps and view disappointments as any open doors for development.
- Strategic connections: Make use of strategic networking to meet influential people. Influence your organization for mentorship, direction, and cooperation.
- Cutting edge Thinking: By anticipating industry trends, cultivate a futuristic mindset. Position yourself to exploit future open doors.
- Online protection Awareness: Remain informed about online protection best practices. Guard your personal information and online presence.
- Creativity and innovation: Cultivate advancement and imagination in critical

thinking. Inspire a culture of trying new things and coming up with new ideas.

- Find a balance between online and offline connections: Keep a harmony between virtual communications and in-person associations. Create authentic online and offline relationships.
- Skills in Data Management: Foster abilities in information to the executives and examination. Comprehend the moral ramifications of information use and security.
- Knowledge of the economy and industry: Keep an eye on changes in your industry and economic trends. Put yourself in a position to adjust to market shifts.
- Global consciousness: Develop worldwide mindfulness and comprehension of assorted viewpoints. Be ready to work in a digital landscape that is globalized and interconnected.

By coordinating these techniques into your expert and individual life, you can adjust, flourish, and make progress in the steadily developing advanced scene. Keep in mind that long-term success in the rapidly changing digital world will depend on one's capacity to adapt to change and continuously acquire new knowledge.

The job of care and flexibility in forming a solid computerized future

Care and flexibility assume essential parts in forming a solid computerized future by encouraging a fair and versatile relationship with innovation. How to do it:

Stress management: Consciousness: Strategies like careful breathing and contemplation can assist people with overseeing pressure related to advanced over-burden.

Resilience: People can overcome stressors and prevent long-term mental health problems by developing resilience.

Digital Health: Consciousness: Empowers purposeful and cognizant utilization of innovation, forestalling thoughtless and inordinate screen time. Responsiveness: aids individuals in overcoming digital obstacles without causing burnout, anxiety, or any other negative effects.

Mindfulness: Raises awareness of interactions that take place online, encourages thoughtful communication, and lowers the likelihood of online disagreements.

Resilience: Teaches people how to deal with cyberbullying and digital conflicts, resulting in healthier online relationships.

Mindfulness: Further develops consideration and focus, alleviating the interruptions that frequently accompany consistent availability. Responsiveness: Assists people with remaining fixed on errands regardless of advanced interruptions, upgrading in general efficiency.

Adjusted Tech Use: Consciousness: Urges people to be aware of their computerized propensities, advancing harmony on the web and disconnected exercises. Responsiveness: enables people to resist the demands of constant connectivity by establishing appropriate limits on technology use.

Capacity to Adapt to Change: Consciousness: encourages people to approach changes in the digital landscape with calm and open minds, which improves adaptability.

Resilience: Develops the ability to deal with and accept technological shifts without becoming overwhelmed or resistant.

Advanced Detox Practices: Consciousness: promotes overall well-being by supporting the adoption of digital detox practices like taking breaks from screens.

Responsible Tech Use: Consciousness: fosters a mindful approach to online behavior and content creation and encourages ethical considerations in technology use.

Anticipation of Advanced Addiction: Consciousness: Brings issues to light of advanced propensities, assisting people with perceiving early indications of habit-forming ways of behaving.

More Effective Decision-Making: Consciousness: reduces the impact of digital distractions on the mind, which in turn improves cognitive clarity and decision-making abilities.

Responsiveness: enables individuals to make decisions based on information and adaptability in the face of digital obstacles.

By coordinating care practices and building versatility, people can add to molding a sound computerized future portrayed by an adjusted, deliberate, and careful commitment to innovation. These characteristics advance a positive computerized culture that focuses on prosperity and moral contemplations.

Conclusion

All in all, developing strength and prosperity in the computerized age is fundamental for exploring the difficulties and potential open doors introduced by innovation. By incorporating care rehearses, people can cultivate a decent connection with computerized gadgets, advancing deliberate and sound tech use. Building strength prepares people to adjust to the steadily advancing computerized scene, alleviating pressure, and quickly returning from misfortunes. In forming a positive computerized future, a proactive way to deal with taking care of oneself, laying out clear limits, and remaining aware of one's computerized propensities assume essential parts. In the end, cultivating resilience and well-being gives people the ability to take advantage of technology's benefits and keep a healthy balance between their digital and real-world lives.

By integrating these central issues and focal points, people can effectively add to forming a positive and versatile computerized future, advancing a solid and offset relationship with innovation.

Encouraging readers to put the principles discussed into practice

- To encourage readers to put the principles of cultivating resilience and well-being in the digital age into practice, it is necessary to emphasize the benefits that can be seen and done and provide steps that can be taken. Here are a few supportive gestures:
- Awareness and empowerment: Stress that developing flexibility and prosperity in the computerized age begins with mindfulness. Urge users to survey their advanced propensities, recognize stressors, and be aware of their profound reactions.
- Careful Tech Engagement: Feature the positive effect of careful tech commitment on emotional wellness. Foster a sense of control and well-being by urging readers to approach their digital interactions with intention.
- Understanding the Effects on Mental Health: Stress the meaning of keeping up with great emotional well-being in the computerized age. Remind readers that practicing resilience and well-being practices improve emotional balance and overall life satisfaction.
- Managing Your Time Online and Offline: Show how it's crucial to strike a balance

between your offline and online activities. Urge users to distribute committed time for non-computerized pursuits, advancing a more comprehensive way of life.

- Developing Positive Digital Habits: Feature the drawn-out advantages of laying out solid advanced propensities. Propel perusers to lay out reasonable objectives for overseeing screen time, diminishing computerized interruptions, and consolidating sans tech customs.

- Providing a Model for Others: Inspire readers to be role models for their families, friends, and peers. Stress the positive impact that developing strength and prosperity can have on the more extensive computerized local area.

- Promoting Relationships' Digital Health: Accentuate how computerized prosperity adds to better connections. Urge users to discuss transparently with loved ones about their advanced limits and back each other in taking on careful tech use.

- Increasing Creativity and Productivity at Work: Feature the association between computerized prosperity and improved efficiency and inventiveness. Inspire users by displaying what a decent way to deal with tech use can decidedly mean for expert and individual achievements.

- Embracing Change and Adaptability: In the digital landscape, encourage an attitude of

- acceptance of change and adaptability. Remind users that developing strength sets them up to explore vulnerabilities and exploit arising open doors.
- Stress Decrease and Work on Mental Health: Show how incorporating strategies for well-being and resilience can reduce stress and improve mental health. Provide testimonials or case studies that demonstrate the transformative effects of employing strategies that are mindful and resilient.
- Observing Little Wins: Remind readers to celebrate the little victories they achieve on their way to digital well-being. Recognize progress and efforts made and encourage a supportive mindset.
- Building a Digitally Friendly Culture: Emphasize individuals' contributions to fostering a positive digital culture. Spur perusers to be advocates for mindful tech use and computerized prosperity inside their networks.

Readers can be inspired and motivated to actively apply the principles of cultivating resilience and well-being in their digital lives by receiving these encouragements. This will ultimately foster a relationship with technology that is healthier and more balanced.

Last considerations on the significance of developing versatility and prosperity in the computerized age

All in all, the significance of developing flexibility and prosperity in the advanced age couldn't possibly be more significant. Mental and emotional well-being must take center stage as we navigate a technological landscape that is changing at a breakneck pace. By effectively taking on rehearses that improve strength and advance prosperity, people engage themselves to confront the difficulties of the computerized period with a feeling of equilibrium and control.

The computerized age offers unbelievable open doors for association, learning, and advancement; however, it likewise presents extraordinary stressors and tensions. Developing versatility furnishes people with the ability to adjust, gain from difficulties, and keep an uplifting perspective notwithstanding computerized difficulties. A mindful and deliberate relationship with technology is made possible by wellness practices, which protect against the negative effects of digital overload and foster a sense of overall contentment.

In addition, cultivating resilience and well-being has a ripple effect that goes beyond the individual benefits. They contribute to the development of a healthier digital culture that is marked by ethical considerations, conscious tech use, and supportive online communities. Embracing these principles becomes a collective responsibility as we collectively shape the future of our digital interactions, fostering a harmonious coexistence with technology.

Putting resources into versatility and prosperity in the computerized age is an interest in a satisfying, adjusted, and feasible lifestyle. It is a journey that requires self-awareness, mindfulness, and the implementation of practical strategies. In the end, it will result in a relationship with the ever-changing digital landscape that is positive and empowers you.